A Vet's

By Liza Charlesworth

ISBN: 978-1-339-02679-4

Art Director: Tannaz Fassihi: Designer: Tanya Chernyak
Photos © Getty Images.

3 4 5 6 7 8 9 10 68 32 31 30 29 28 27 26 25 24

Printed in Jiaxing, China. First printing, August 2023.

SCHOLASTIC

It is a vet and a pet.
A vet's job is to help pets.

A kid's cat is sick.
A vet can help it get well.

A dog's leg has a bump on it.
A vet can fix it quick.

A vet can see a pig.
She will help it get big.

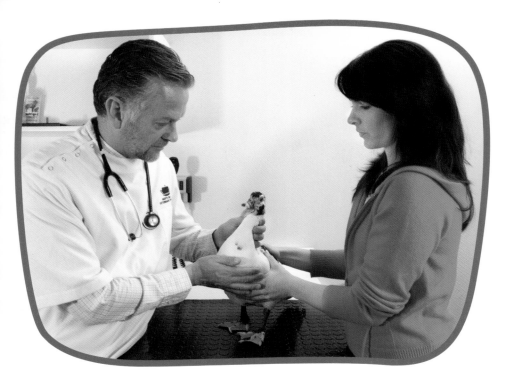

A vet can see a duck.
He will help it to quack.

Can a vet fix a pup's cut?
Yes! The pup is so glad.

A vet's job is to help pets.
A vet is the best!